Portuguese
Memory
Book

Portuguese Memory Book

A New Approach to Vocabulary Building

William F. Harrison and
Dorothy Winters Welker

University of Texas Press
Austin

Requests for permission to reproduce material from this
work should be sent to Permissions, University of Texas
Press, P.O. Box 7819, Austin, TX 78713-7819

∞ The paper used in this publication meets the minimum
requirements of American National Standard for Information Sciences—Permanence of Paper for Printed Library
Materials, ANSI Z39.48-1984.

Library of Congress Cataloging-in-Publication Data

Harrison, William F., 1934–
    Portuguese memory book : a new approach to vocabu-
lary building / by William F. Harrison and Dorothy
Winters Welker. — 1st ed.
        p.   cm.
    ISBN 0-292-73105-1 (cl.: alk. paper). —
    ISBN 0-292-73106-X (pbk.: alk. paper)
    1. Portuguese language—Vocabulary. 2. Portuguese
language—Provincialisms—Brazil—Rio de Janeiro.
I. Welker, Dorothy Winters, 1905–   . II. Title.
PC5256.H37   1996
469.81—dc20   96-11038

CONTENTS

INTRODUCTION

This book will introduce you to Brazilian Portuguese, the language spoken in the South American country of Brazil. Many Portuguese dialects are heard in that vast country. Of these, the Carioca dialect of Rio de Janeiro is one of the most popular, and is the dialect that is used in this book.

In dealing with any new language, one of the first things you will want to do is to acquire a stock of useful words that you can recognize and pronounce easily. The *Portuguese Memory Book* shows you how to accomplish this task quickly and effortlessly. It enables you to recognize many Portuguese words when you see or hear them (passive vocabulary), and to recall these words when you speak or write (active vocabulary). Although the Portuguese heard in Portugal is somewhat different from that of Brazil, you will be able to understand the peninsular version after you have become familiar with Brazilian Portuguese.

The *Portuguese Memory Book* is about vocabulary, and vocabulary only. That is why it can help you learn vocabulary so fast. It is not a textbook on grammar. If you are interested in learning Portuguese grammar, you should consult a teacher of Brazilian Portuguese or a good grammar textbook.

The *Portuguese Memory Book* shows you how to use mnemonic devices to learn vocabulary. A mnemonic device sets up an association between a new word and one or more familiar words that enables you to recall the new word easily. Mnemonic devices are not new, of course; they have been used for centuries. We still call upon them every day to help us remember names, numbers, and many other things: "Spring forward in the spring; fall back in the fall" is one example. The mnemonic devices used in the *Portuguese Memory Book* are short jingles that present the <u>pronunciation</u> of a Portuguese word along with the English <u>meaning</u> of that word. They fairly jingle the new words into your memory.

Research has shown, surprisingly enough, that the more far-fetched, even absurd, a mnemonic device is, the better it helps you remember. You will probably agree that many of the jingles in the *Portuguese Memory Book* qualify for high marks in absurdity. You will enjoy learning and applying them.

The *Portuguese Memory Book* contains mnemonic jingles for more than 500 words useful for conversation and reading. Most of these words have been culled from the American Council of Education's *A Graded Word Book of Brazilian Portuguese* (Brown et al., 1945), a standard work that is still a valuable compendium. Additional words were taken from contemporary textbooks.

HOW TO USE THE
Portuguese Memory Book

Each jingle in this book gives you two pieces of information about a Portuguese word: 1) its sound (pronunciation, including stress, or accent), and 2) its sense (meaning). The jingle uses the word in a natural setting that helps you store in your memory both the sound and the sense of the word. You need not memorize an entire lyric. Just remember the significant parts.

The following jingle will show you how the method works.

noite (f.)   night

Don't an**noy Chi**huahuas in the **night**.
If you ignore their bark, you'll feel their bite.

The Portuguese word to be learned is noite. The English equivalent of noite is "night," which is in boldface type in the jingle. The sound of noite is given by the last syllable of an**noy** plus the first syllable of **Chi**huahua. In the jingle, the syllables **noy** and **Chi** are printed in boldface type and underscored. These two syllables, read together, spell out the sound of the complete Portuguese word noite. Note that here, as always in this book, the English sounds used to spell out the sound of the Portuguese word are consecutive. That makes them easy to recognize and to remember. The meter for each jingle was chosen so that the accent falls on the stressed syllable of the Portuguese word.

Here is another example:

coelho   rabbit

That **quail you** see has non-fowl habits.
She likes to play around with **rabbits**.

The sound and stress of Portuguese coelho are given by
quail plus **you**.

CONVENTIONS USED
IN THIS BOOK

As far as possible, the jingles reproduce the sounds and stresses of the Portuguese words. Three Brazilian sounds require special treatment: 1) nasalized vowels and diphthongs; 2) r in certain combinations; 3) s in certain combinations. These are explained below:

1. In Portuguese, vowels and diphthongs can be either plain or nasalized. A nasalized vowel is produced when air is allowed to resonate in the nose as well as in the mouth. Example: plain vowel, moo; nasalized vowel, moon. Portuguese nasalized vowels and diphthongs are more highly nasalized than nasalized sounds in English.

In this book a nasalized vowel is indicated by an italicized *m* or *n* following the vowel. These italicized letters are not pronounced. Example:

mu*n*do   earth, world

Look at the **moon. Do** you know why
It follows the **earth** around the sky?

The sound of mu*n*do is given by the moo of **moon** plus **Do**. In this book the italicized *n* is simply a signal that the oo of moo is to be nasalized. (In certain words, such as mu*n*do, a faint suggestion of an n can be heard in the background.)

2. The r between vowels or in consonant clusters (pr, br, dr, tr, cr, gr, fr) has the sound of the tt, in American English potty. Here is an example:

choro   weeping, sobbing (n.)

The **show rou**tinely ends with **weeping**,
At least for all who still aren't sleeping.

The sound of the Portuguese word is captured by the word show followed by the rou of routinely. As the rule just given requires, the r in choro is pronounced like the tt in potty. This r is left unmarked.

When r is not between vowels and is not in a consonant cluster it has the sound of a highly exaggerated h (approximating the Spanish j). In this book this sound is indicated by an italicized *r* in bold print. Here is an example:

*r*ouba*r*   to rob

You must p**robe Ar**thur's links with crime.
He **robbed** his Ma of her last dime.

The sound of *r*ouba*r* is built up from the sound of robe in p**r**obe plus A**r** of A**r**thur's. Both the initial and the final *r* of *r*ouba*r* have the sound of a highly exaggerated h.

3. The letter s has several sounds in Carioca Portuguese, depending on its environment in a word. Before the sounds p, t, k, and at the end of a breath group, s has the sound of sh in shirt. In this book the sh sound is represented by an italicized *s*. Here is an example:

bi*s*po   bishop

Bee, *s*poon out some applesauce;
The **Bishop** lost his dental floss!

In this jingle, the sound of the Portuguese word is captured by the underscored syllables. As was noted above, the italicized *s* is pronounced like the sh in shirt.

For a more extensive view of the sounds of Carioca Portuguese, refer to the pronunciation guide in the Appendix.

OTHER CONVENTIONS

1. The main Portuguese entry always gives the infinitive of verbs and the singular of nouns. The pronunciation demonstrated in the jingle applies to these basic forms. In the jingle the English equivalent of the Portuguese entry may appear in any convenient form. For example, a verb may be in any tense, and a noun may be either singular or plural.

2. The gender of nouns is given except for nouns ending in o (which are usually masculine), or in a (usually feminine). Endings in o and a are given for adjectives that indicate gender by these vowels.

3. In the jingles, a long dash [—] may indicate a change of speaker.

VOCABULARY

abafar   to stifle, choke, smother

Bob, a farmer, finds he cannot **stifle**
His little son's desire to own a rifle.
So why deny the youngster such a trifle?

abraço   embrace, hug (n.)

A bra, **Sue**, should define a form with grace,
Nor should it sag or split in my **embrace**.

abrasar   to burn

Bob, Roz ardently desires
To burn herself in sacred fires,
But still thinks poets all are liars.

abrir   to open

To open the debating season,
Bob reared a monument to reason.

aceitar   to accept

Ah, say tarpon strikes your fancy.
I can't **accept** a dish so chancy!
Just order Spam for me and Nancy.

acen der   to set fire to, turn on

Ah, send aeronauts as brave as these
To no insane aggressors overseas
Who **set a fire to** everything they please!

acertar   to hit upon

Ross, air Tarzan's dark and shameful deed.
Then **hit upon** a way to make him bleed!

achar   to think, believe, find

I **think a shar**per sword has never torn me
Than this your smile that tells how much you scorn me.

açougue (m.)   butchershop, meat market, slaughterhouse

Ah, so guitar-like is the hawker's voice
The products of his **butchershop** seem choice!

açúcar (m.)   sugar

Ah, Sue, careers can turn out sweet as **sugar**
Even for me, an ordinary bugger.

adeus   farewell

Am**adeus** was his middle name—
Mozart, who never said **farewell** to fame.

adiar   to postpone

Ah, gee, Arthur! Please **postpone**
Your scolding while I use the phone!

adubo   fertilizer, manure

Ah, do boot Harry off the vaudeville stage!
Pelt him with **fertilizer**, rocks, and rage!

agrícola   agricultural
    (adj., m. or f.)

We **agree Cola** truly tastes great
On a hot **agricultural** date.

água   water

Man**agua water** tastes like death.
That's why there's whiskey on my breath!

aí   there

Ah, even though you do not care,
It helps to know you're always **there**!

ain da   yet, still

Ah, e'en Dakotas cannot quite forget
The tepees in their wake are smoking **yet**.

ala   wing (of a building)

La S**cala**'s added on a special **wing**
Where you and other amateurs can sing.

alegre   happy, merry

Ah, lay green ferns within the airy nest
Where **happy**, but endangered, birdlings nest.

além   beyond, over there (adv.)

A lame attempt to trick us and abscond
Has lured our foe to seek the great **beyond**.

algum, -a   some

N**ow, goo m**ay hold that silly wig in place,
But **some**thing drastic's needed for your face!

alho   garlic

D**oll, you** gobble such a lot of **gar-**
-Lic, I prefer that you remain afar.

ali   there

A leotard looks very nice on Annie.
See **there**? She has a decorative fanny!

alime*n*tar   to feed

Ollie mea*n*t Arthur **to feed** her pet cat.
But Arthur likes catfood, the treacherous brat!

alime*n*to   food

Ollie mea*n*t to change her attitude
And cease to spend her pay on high-priced **food**.

alma   soul

Upon your br**ow, Ma**tilda, ever lies
The imprint of a **soul** in Paradise.
And so I find my heaven in your eyes.

almoço   lunch

W**ow**! **Moe sou**ped up his old jalopy!
Still, as a site for **lunch**, it's sloppy.

alto, -a   high, tall

For denim pants and shirts I have a passion.
But these days all must b**ow to high**-style fashion!

aluno, -a   student

Ah, Lou, new students need to learn
That candles have two ends to burn.

amar   to love

Who **loves a mar**tyr loves a fool!
So calm your ardor, keep your cool.

amarrar   to moor, tie up

Ah, Ma harbors foolish expectations
Of **mooring** boats for these United Nations!

amassar   to crush, pound

—**Mama, Ser**geant Gore **has** almost **crushed**
My lips. —Well, darling, it's because you gushed.

ambos   both

T**om boos**ts ardently his famous twin.
They **both** were born to play the game and win.

amigo, -a   friend

—**Ah, me! goo** rolls from every pore.
—**Friend**, sleep it off, and drink no more.

amo   master

Ah, moo soft and sweetly, gentle friend.
Your **master**'s bull is just around the bend.

amor (m.)   love

A mortal wholly lacking **love**
Is like a hand without a glove.

andar (m.)   floor, story (of a building)

Don darling, we shall need a top-**floor** bedroom
So our giraffe will have a lot of headroom.

andar   to walk

On Dartmouth campus once I **walked**.
I liked the way the students talked.

ano   year

Don't look so w**an, Nu**reen. A few more sprints
And you'll be seen in this **year**'s racing prints!

apaga**r**   to turn off (lights, stove)

Our p**apa guar**ds his children's health
And **turns off** lights to save their wealth.

ape**rta**r   to squeeze

M**a, pair Tar**zan with petite Suzanne.
I know he'd like **to squeeze** her if he can!

apre**n**de**r**   to learn

A t**op wren dare**s, no doubt, **to learn**
To fly to France when it comes her turn.

apura**r** (1)   to find out

Ah, poor Art! He's trying **to find out**
Why so much talent brings so little clout.

apura**r** (2)   to perfect

Ah, poor Arthur! He just can't **perfect**
His plan to fool the president-elect!

aquele, aquela   that (previously mentioned),
                                that (over yonder)

Ah, **Kelly** must and Kelly can
Design and carry out a plan.
And **that** will prove the guy's a man.

aqui   here

Ah, **key** your spending to your wages,
And you will flourish **here** for ages.

a**r** (m.)   air

Never **ar**gue with your spouse.
Just let fresh **air** into the house,
And say you acted like a louse.

a**r**de**r**   to burn

I know you **burn** to, but you simply can't
Ba**r** **Der**ek's visits to your maiden aunt.

areia   sand

A ray of hope has touched these barren lands.
Once more the children play upon the **sands**.

ari**s**co, -a   surly, aloof, suspicious

Ah, Reese, **coo**l off! You're big and burly.
What devil makes you look so **surly**?

a**r**ma   gun, weapon

We'll **arm a** nation with tanks and ships,
And pile up **guns** till the enemy flips.

arra*s*ta*r*   to drag

Minneh**aha**, *s***tar**ved for love, began
To drag her steps. But then she found her man!

arremete*r*   to attack, assail

Ah, **hey**! **may Ter**ry not **attack** you
Till we can find a gang to back you!

arroz (m.)   rice

"**Ahoy**!" **sh**e cried. "I've brought the **rice**.
Your lively crew will add the spice."

asa   wing (of a bird)

Ah, wounded bird upon the pl**aza**, sing
The piteous story of your broken **wing**!

a*s*pira*r*   to inhale

Ah, *s***pear Ar**thur! Better yet,
Make him **inhale** a cigarette!

assi*m*   thus, so

Berta **see***m*s too wise to make a fuss,
So can you tell me why she's scowling **thus**?

assi*s*ti*r*   to attend

Ah, **cea***s***e chee***r*ing for a football team
That won't **attend** a course in self-esteem!

assu*s*ta*r*   to frighten

Pa, **Sue** *s***tar**s in many a gangster movie.
It **frightens** me, but she declares it's groovy!

atar   to tie up, tie

The cops g<u>ot Tar</u>zan. First they **tied** him **up**,
But later found him harmless as a pup.

até   until

The hot p<u>até</u> upon my plate
Was fine **until** I overate.

ate*n*der   to heed, answer (telephone), be attentive to

<u>Ah</u>, **ten**d Er</u>ic while he's sick.
Heed his needs, and make it quick!

ato   act

<u>Ah! **too**</u> oft your **acts** have brought disgrace
Upon our justly celebrated race.

atual   present (adj.)

I gave my P<u>a **two ow**</u>ls I chanced to capture.
His **present** state is something less than rapture.

aula   class, course

How did the <u>**owl a**</u>cquire his reputation
In all the college **classes** of the nation?

aurora   dawn

<u>**N**ow **roar a**</u> while, and get it off your chest.
When comes the **dawn**, you'll find your mom knows best.

averiguar   to inquire, examine

I'll serve <u>**a very Guar**</u>ani-like meal
If you'll **inquire** about some roasted eel.

avô   grandfather

A vote for my **grandfather** tells the town
You favor a mayor who won't back down.

avó   grandma, grandmother

I found **a vau**nted recipe
My **grandma** tried to hide from me.

barato, -a   cheap

Club rules **bar ah! too** many from our not-so-**cheap** society,
When all that's really needed is a minimal sobriety.

ba*r*ba   beard

A **ba*r*ba**rous practice, greatly feared,
Is shaving off a convict's **beard**.

barriga   belly, stomach

See Ab**ba. He go**t jam and jelly,
Stuffed once more his bulging **belly**.

bas*ta*r   to be enough

Ab**ba *sta***rred—and flopped—in his first show.
That **was enough** to use up all his dough.

bebe*r*   to drink

Give the **babe ai*r***! Make her **drink** water!
After all, boys, she's somebody's daughter!

bebida   drink (n.)

Bom**bay Bee, D**ot's favorite **drink**,
First turns her purple, then bright pink!

beijo   kiss

The color **beige U**lrike often wears
Has brought her hugs and **kisses** (so she swears).

beira   brim, edge, lip, rim

I o**bey Ra**mona's every whim
And fill her coffee mug up to the **brim**.

bélico, -a   warlike, belligerent

The **belle Lee coo**lly courted was low in worldly treasures,
But prettily responsive to his rather **warlike** measures.

belo, -a   beautiful, fair

The jealous **belle—Lou**ella—gave an order
To trash her rival's **beautiful** recorder.

be*m*   well, fine

Bemby's doing rather **well**.
He even wrote some books that sell!

bicho   beastie; any unspecified animal, insect, or
               worm

—How does a **bee shoo** rival swarms from his ancestral hive?
—He stings the pesky **beasties**. Then he captures them alive.

bi*s*po   bishop

Bee, *s*poon out some applesauce:
The **Bishop** lost his dental floss!

boca   mouth

A **beau co**llapsed somewhere down south.
His girlfriend slapped him in the **mouth**.

boi   steer, ox

A **boi**sterous herd of **steers** paraded through the stadium.
They couldn't be more joyful if they'd just discovered radium!

bola   ball

Let them **bawl a**while, that noisy crowd
Of foot**ball** fans less well informed than loud!

bo*m*, boa   good

You know, a little **bon e** is **good** for puppies.
Just so, a little bonus pleases yuppies.

briga*r*   to come to blows, fight

Bo**b regar**ded faithless Rose:
"And so at last we **come to blows!**"

brisa   breeze

Brie's a jolly picnic cheese,
Fresh and fragrant on the **breeze**.

brota*r*   to bud

Bo**b wrote Tar**zan in his own red blood:
"The seeds of vengeance ever swell and **bud!**"

bruma   fog, mist

Take a **broom, a**ttack my room,
And sweep it clear of **fog** and gloom.

busca   search (n.)

Let's end the futile **search** for maybe's and perhapses,
And plan how we can save our skins when this ca**boose**
collapses.

buscar   to get, bring, fetch

Bam**boo scar**s are mostly not too serious.
But **get** a doctor if you feel delirious.

cá   here

Cobblestones are pretty hard on bikes,
So folks who live **here** mostly go on hikes.

cabeça   head

Don't let the In**ca base a** camp
Here where the ground is cold and damp.
His **head** will ache, his legs will cramp,
He'll be as soilworn as a tramp.

caber   to fit into, be contained in

The In**ca bur**ied deep his trusty bow
To fit into the world that white men know.

cada   each

We must eat **cod a** time or two **each** day
Until this long recession goes away.

cadeira   seat, chair

A buc**k a day Ro**d laid away, and so it's far from strange
Last week he bought a proper **seat** upon the Stock Exchange.

caderno   notebook

The In**ca dare new** paths to tread—
They're bleeding as their fathers bled.
This **notebook** lists the noble dead.

caipira (m. or f.)   yokel, hillbilly

Jac**k, I peer a**cross the fence.
Saves me a ticket at fifty cents—
To a local **yokel** a sum immense.

calor (m.)   heat, warmth

—The **heat**'s on. Fis**cal or**der is a must.
—So bring your files. But first, wipe off the dust.

cama   bed

Commas help us get our sentence said,
Periods let us spend our time in **bed**,
And exclamation points demand, "Drop dead!"

câmara   chamber, room

It doesn't be**come a ra**bbinical student to think
His spacious, luxurious **chambers** decidedly stink!

caminho   road

And did the In**ca mean, You** know the **road**
From city lights to his despised abode?

canela   cinnamon

Dor**ca, Nell a**grees to post a sign:
"**Cinnamon** drops! A nickel gets you nine!"

caneta   pen

Dun**can ate a** grasshopper, and then he took a **pen**
And wrote his Ma he never would do such a thing again.

cansar   to tire

It **tires** me out to see the congregation
Applaud this i**con**, **Ser**geant Carr's creation.

cantar   to sing

Her smiles **con Tar**zan into **singing**
And start his great gorillas swinging.

cara   face

My **car a**gain has lost a race.
It just exploded in my **face**!

careta   "face," grimace

Os**car ate a** fish somewhat decayed.
He said no word, but what a **face** he made!

carga   load, cargo

Our **car ga**lumphed along the road
Till we could dump our grisly **load**.

carinho   love (n.)

To show your **love**, **careen** Eulalia's boat and paint the hull.
But guard it from the calling-card of every passing gull!

carne (f.)   meat

—The **car Ne**al sold me smells of rancid **meat**.
—He used to peddle burgers on the street.

caro, -a   dear, expensive

The **car rou**tinely calls for me at seven.
And if you drive, **dear** girl, it's very Heaven!

carta   letter

The mailman has to **cart a** lot of **letters**
From creditors to unrepentant debtors.

casa   house

Franti**c Ah's a**ccompanied the singing.
With cries of "Bravo!" too the **house** was ringing.

catar   to search

I fear a mild **catar**rh will trouble those
Who **searched** the icy bog and almost froze.

cebola   onion

They all **say Bo la**mented (I find it rather funny)
The smell of **onions** in our town, but not the smell of money!

cedo   early

We **say, Do** everything that any one of us can think of
To put an **early** end to this ordeal we're on the brink of.

cédula   bank note, decree, permit

Sed, do lamentable creatures like you
Ever get hold of a **bank note** or two?

ceia   supper

Say ya have some friends come in for **supper**:
Of course you'll give each one a picker-upper!

cem   hundred

The **same** old gags, the same old foolish faces
Have bored me in a **hundred** different places.

cena   stage, scene

A **sane a**pproach to going on the **stage**
Is: Wait until you're clearly over-age.

ce**r**to, -a   sure

A careless **heir to** bonds and stocks
Is **sure** to end up on the rocks.

cessa**r**   to cease

I don't **say so**rry crooks—such men as I and you—
Should **cease** to live. But isn't that the decent thing to do?

chá (m.)   tea

—We shall have to **sho**p for **tea**.
—A simple coke will do for me.

chama**r**   to call

Men ru**sh a mar**tyr to the fire
That **calls** him to his heart's desire.

chega**r**   to arrive

Shay guards his manly right to curse
His ever late-**arriving** nurse.

choca**r**   to hit, smash into; shock

Show Carlos how to drive a car
Before he **hits** another bar.

choro   weeping, crying, sobbing (n.)

Our **show rou**tinely ends with **weeping**,
At least for all who still aren't sleeping.

chove**r**   to rain

The braves **show ver**y little pain
When in their lives it starts **to rain**!

cidade (f.)   city

See Dodge eat up our **city**'s meager money—
His Honor's taking trips to woo his honey!

cima   peak, summit

—**See Ma**tilda scale that lofty **peak**!
—If she can make it, that's the girl I seek.

ci**n**tura   waistline

Have you **seen two ra**bbinical guys,
With **waistlines** both of the largest size?

coelho   rabbit

That **quail you** see has non-fowl habits.
She likes to play around with **rabbits**.

coisa   thing

Coy's a word I've scarcely heard.
Is it a beast, a **thing**, a bird?

cólera   anger

Cole, ere Adele explodes in **anger**,
Hustle her off to her friends in Bangor.

colocar   to put, place

Cole, oh! cart away your junk.
Don't **put** it underneath my bunk!

co**m**   with

The **com**b **with** which I once arranged your curls
Seems now more precious than ancestral pearls.

come**r**   to eat

The cox**comb, heir** to Grandpa's wealth,
Just **ate** all day and wrecked his health.

comete**r**   to commit

Comb a terrorist and find a sadist.
Of all bad actions, he **commits** the baddest!

como   like, as, how

The **Comb Oo**na gave me I'm saving for Gus.
It's much too bejewelled for poor folk **like** us.

comove**r**   to rouse

Coe, mow very gingerly. It's easy
To rouse the rattlesnakes and make them queasy.

co**n**strui**r**   to build

Cohn**, strew eer**ie glances 'round the room
To **build** an atmosphere of dread and doom!

co**n**tra   against

The ice cream **co**n**e tra**versed a ten-inch gap
And crashed **against** the Flight Commander's lap.

corpo   body

The s**core Pu**laski High School mustered
Has left the student **body** flustered.

corrida   race

Co**co, heed a** friendly warning;
The rat **race** starts anew each morning.

cortar   to cut

No en**core Tar**zan got, since they had **cut**
A scene much celebrated for its smut.

costa   coast, shore

The **cost of** forts along the **coast**
Will profit some, but anger most.

crescer   to grow

Let's have a tal**k race, Sar**ah. As we **grow**,
We'll tell each other everything we know.

crise (f.)   crisis

The court de**crees**: "E**ject** the killer ants
Which in this **crisis** fled to Papa's pants!"

cru, crua   raw, crude

Raw re**cru**its, lick my boots!
Stand and practice your salutes!

cruz (f.)   cross

S**crewy Sh**irley's not a total loss.
She's learned to mark her paycheck with a **cross**.

cruzar   to cruise

Cruise ardently about your native seas.
Some day you'll **cruise** the far Antipodes.

daí   hence, thence

Ada eats too much, and **hence**
Has rapidly become immense.

danado, -a   damned, cursed

Don, ah! do all you feel you must and can!
You may be **damned**, but you'll become a man!

dançar   to dance

Don sorry pants and grimy shirt
To dance the dance we call "The Dirt."

dar   to give

Darla, **give** to Tom your best,
And leave for others all the rest.

datar   to give the date of

Dot argued, she could count on Women's Lib
To **date** the speech in which you told a fib.

de   from, of

E**uge**ne one day, to keep **from** being bored,
Stirred up the vassals **of** his feudal lord.

dedo   finger, toe

Every **day do finger** exercises,
And then your flute will bring you few surprises.

deferir   to approve, grant

One **day Fay rear**ed her pretty head and snorted,
"I don't **approve** of strolling unescorted!"

defesa   defense

You each **day phase a** program out.
Your sole **defense**, "I've lost my clout!"

deitar   to lay

Date Arthur if you want **to lay**
Your head upon a bed of hay.

descolar   to unglue

Des, Cole argued loud and long.
He came **unglued** when proved dead wrong!

descuidar   to neglect, overlook

O little **desk, wee dar**ling of my youth,
You taught me never **to neglect** the truth.

desligar   to unloose, unfasten

Dez, Lee guards the secret with his life—
How he **unloosed** your boat without a knife.

despertar   to waken

Waken Dess, pare tartar off her teeth,
And show the costly dentures underneath!

dever   to owe; ought

I **owe** this gentle warning to my mother:
Each **day var**ies slightly from another:
Yesterday we froze. Today we smother.

dez   ten

The **day sh**e owned she loved me not
Ten rivals claimed her on the spot.

dia (m.)   day

Gee! **a** new idea hits me every **day**.
Sometimes I almost wish that it would go away!

dis car   to dial (telephone)

Mar**gie scar**s her pretty face with scowls,
And when she **dials** the telephone, she growls.

dizer   to say, tell

Mar**gie's air** is somewhat stiff and haughty.
They **say** it comes from never being naughty.

doce   sweet

The **dose 'e** took seemed **sweet** and good.
And yet it failed 'im where 'e stood.

doer   to suffer, ache, feel pain

Do**do air**ily observed,
"All my angles, sir, are curved."
(And yet she **suffers**, we're aware,
From liver spots and falling hair.)

domar   to tame, subdue

O Wal**do, mar**k my words: I'll **tame** you,
And end these rages that inflame you!

dona   lady

This **dough no**t only fills the **lady**'s need:
It satisfies her ever-growing greed.

do*r* (m.)   pain, suffering

Slam the **door** on **pain** and sorrow—
Plenty more will come tomorrow!

do*r*mi*r*   to sleep

This **door mere**ly guards the castle keep.
Our ghost lives there to haunt you while you **sleep**.

duvida*r*   to doubt

Doovy, **dar**ling, fetch my sweater,
Pick my bag up, mail my letter.
Doubt not, you're my best go-getter!

e   and

W**e**'ve tied together with a word
The rational **and** the absurd.

ela   she

In a c**ell a** prisoner can glory
That in the scandal-sheets **she**'ll read her story.

ele   he

D**ale ea**ts more than cousin Ellie.
He scares her with his bulging belly.

e*m*   at, in, on

McL**ain at** gambling is a shark.
Just how he wins? I'm **in** the dark.

embora   although, though

You helped th**em bore a** tunnel through the hill,
Although you knew their purpose was to kill.

ensinar   to teach

B**en, seen ar**guing so oft, or preaching,
Just cannot learn if someone else is **teaching**.

ensino   instruction, training

M**en see new** reason to provide **instruction**
For kids who want to learn to raise a ruction.

então   then

Wh**en town** seems just too far for man or dog,
Sigh, **then** watch a TV travelogue.

entender   to understand

Wh**en ten dare to understand**,
Nine will fight and one command.

entre   among, between

Among the ge**ntry** you'll detect with scorn
Deceit in persons to the manor born.

época   time, epoch

Did S**ep poke a** thumb in your innocent face?
It's a sign of the man and the **time** and the place.

equipe (m.)   staff, team

You men m**ay keep ea**ch one a **staff** of butlers if you wish.
Just make them sniff and taste each day of every doubtful dish.

escalar   to climb, scale

Be**ss, call Ar**t **to climb** the garden wall.
We'll get those melons now or not at all.

escola   school

L**es, call a** waiter, order something cool.
Now—isn't this a lot more fun than **school**?

esconder   to hide, conceal

Y**es, Cohn, dare** to throw your weight around.
Just **hide** your fears and learn to hold your ground.

esfera   sphere

Le**ss fair a** girl at once appeared to be
When she declared her **sphere** included me.

esforço   effort, endeavor

—L**es, force** Ulrika, can't you, to be a bit more gentle?
—Such an **effort** can't succeed. She'd think me sentimental.

esperança   hope (n.)

Be**ss, spare Ron** sufficient dough
To give us **hope** he'll pack and go.

esperar   to wait for, except, hope

Y**es, spare ar**tless tax evaders
Who **wait** in vain **for** Nader's Raiders.

esperto, -a   clever

If we, L**es, spare too** many lawless guys,
Those **clever** thugs will stage our quick demise.

esquecer   to forget

In formal dr**ess, Kay cer**emoniously bowed,
Forgetting she was scorned by almost all her crowd.

esquivar   to shun, avoid

The p**esky var**mint deftly **shuns**
The sight and sound of lawmen's guns.

esse, essa   that (just mentioned), that (near listener)
                                 (adj.)

The l**ess 'e** knows of what took place
The less 'e'll share in **that** disgrace.

estar   to be (temporarily)

I **was le**ss star**tled than I had expected.
I simply had the would-be thief ejected.

este, esta   this (adj.)

T**ess, cheat** on. **This** trait of yours
Is shared, I find, by bums and boors.

estender   to stretch out, extend

Be**ss, tend Er**ic as you did before:
Just **stretch** the drunkard **out** and let him snore.

estirpe (f.)   stock, ancestry, lineage

L**es, cheer Pe**tunia up. Although of humble **stock**
She knows full well what fork to choose and how to use a wok.

estrela   star

Be**ss, trail a star** across the sky.
You'll catch its sparkle in your eye.

evita**r**   shun, avoid

Evvie, tar and feather those
Who **shun** the use of underclothes.

fala**r**   to talk, speak

Wol**f, alar**med at what I told him,
Wouldn't **talk** for fear I'd scold him.

farol (m.)   beacon, headlight

Upon the so**fa ro**ll the kids at play,
Each one a **beacon** for a brighter day.

fa**r**to, -a   glutted, full

Far too many highways, sleek and **glutted**,
On crooked, rain-washed country roads abutted.

fato   fact

If ah! too many citizens should learn too many **facts**,
A lot of guys in politics would answer for their acts.

ferido, -a   wounded

Jef**f, a re-do** of your condo wouldn't cost too much.
Will you feel **wounded** if I try to add a woman's touch?

feri**r**   to wound

Fay, rear your lovely head. You swooned
When someone tried your love **to wound**!

fe**s**ta   party

The fe**st a**ppeared to be a great success.
But every **party** leaves the house a mess—
Especially when half the guests undress.

fiar (1)   to sell on credit

Du**ffy ar**gued vainly when I said it:
"To you I can't and will not **sell on credit**."

fiar (2)   to vouch for

When Du**ffy ar**gues loud and long,
I'll **vouch for** it that he'll be wrong.

ficar   to remain

The "Date-a-Star" **fee Car**a gets
Remains too high for jobless vets.

ficha   token; index card

The **fee Char**lene demands is just a **token**
Of all the many promises she's broken.

figura   figure, countenance, shape

The ta**ffy goo Ra**mona often ate
Enlarged her **figure** to a forty-eight.

filho   son

Son, I feel you hardly know me well
Enough to greet me with "You go to hell!"

fim (m.)   end

—My **fem**ur seems so stiff!—Well, in the **end**
No one can teach a thigh-bone how to bend.

fita   ribbon, tape

The **fee To**m charges seems a bit unfair
For simply hanging **ribbons** in my hair.

flor (f.)   flower

If Lord Augustus called us to his side,
We came, our native country's **flower** and pride,
Not really caring if we lived or died.

floresta   jungle

Just let **Flo rest a** while, till she agrees
She cannot see the **jungle** for the trees.

fora   outside (adv.)

When **four a**ttractive office girls applied,
I asked the fifth and sixth to wait **outside**.

força   force (n.)

Four sabbatical trips he made.
With almost all his expenses paid.
The Air **Force** suddenly feels betrayed,
And wishes he'd gone to France and stayed!

formiga   ant

Form eager lines before the coke machine
Like **ants** competing to escort their queen.

forno   furnace, oven

Four new furnaces the Army hastened to install.
Here faint and freezing refugees lined up from wall to wall.

foro   bar (law), forum

Four rheumatic lawyers, long banished from the **bar**,
Sneak around and wonder where the free refreshments are.

frango   chicken

If **Ron**, **gou**rmet authority on dining,
Approves the **chicken**, we can stop repining.

frea**r**   to restrain, brake, curb

But **if Ray ar**dently desires
To marry, why **restrain** his fires?

frita**r**   to fry

Free Tarzan from his willow bond,
And **fry** that steak of which he's fond.
But watch him lest he should abscond!

fruta   fruit

If **ruta**baga gives you gas,
Eat some **fruit** and it will pass.

fu**n**dar   to base, found

Where once a ty**phoon dar**kened sky and sea
We **based** our camp, with glamor, guts, and glee.

futebol (m.)   soccer

Foo Chee Baw's the way to yell it.
That means **soccer**. Who dares spell it?

gaba**r**   to extol, praise

Your to**ga bar**s you from our swimming pool.
So back to Rome, O Caesar. Play it cool!
We can **extol** your style, but not your rule.

galho   branch

Cha**gall, you** flower of Russia and of France,
Would you could paint this trembling willow **branch**!

galo   cock, rooster

Cha**gall lu**red Jacqueline to try to paint,
So now she pictures all the things she ain't—
A **cock**, a hen, a sinner, and a saint,
Plus nameless things that make us want to faint.

garbo   gallantry, grace

His **garb, ou**tré for all its gold and lace,
Hardly enhanced his **gallantry** and grace.

garfo   fork

Your big ci**gar foo**led little Teddy.
He brought a **fork** to hold it steady.

gato   cat

We've **got to** train our **cat**
To scoot when we say "Scat!"

gostar   to enjoy, like

Sue, **go star** in yet another foolish movie.
I shan't **enjoy** it, but your Ma will find it groovy.

gostoso, -a   savory, delicious, tasty

Go stow Zuleika's luggage in cellar or in attic,
Then feed her something **savory** and yet aristocratic.

gota   drop

Go, **To**m, get a kitchen mop.
On my floor you've spilled a **drop**!

gra**n**de   great, big

Bi**g Ron jee**red wildly as he gulped and tried to hide:
"I ate some **great** big devils, and I think they're still inside!"

grasnada   croak, caw, quack

My do**g Raj nodde**d quickly off to sleep on
A log some frogs, with **croaks**, began to leap on.

grita**r**   to shout, scream

Greet Tarzan, climbing down the tree.
Just **shout** and **scream**, and so will he.

gua**r**da**r**   to keep

The Ja**guar**, **dar**ling, you can **keep** for free.
Our other cars the judge assigned to me.

guia (m. or f.)   guide

Mc**Gee a**ppears to need a **guide**
Through this uncharted countryside.

have**r**   to have (aux.)

Ah! **ver**y often I **have** thought
I'd start to do the things I ought.
But one thing I am sure I know:
Thinking doesn't make it so!

homem   man

"Home" embraces, doubtless, many kinds of "sweet."
But none have meaning for a **man** who's living on the street.

hora   hour

Give me an **hour, or a** moment at least,
And try not to roar like a ravening beast!

igual   same, equal

OUR **league wow**ed MacArthur's league!
He swears he scents a base intrigue!
To you and me it's all the **same**,
For in the end it's just a game.

ilha   island, isle

The **island eel ya** caught with such exertion
Will doubtless be enhanced by long immersion.

ir   to go

The words you lavish on my brother
Go in one **ear** and out the other.

ira   wrath

O sixties, **era** fraught with righteous **wrath**,
'Twas you that taught me manners, mirth, and math!

irmão   brother

We all h**ear Mau M**au **brothers** rudely wrangle
About the latest diplomatic tangle.

janela   window

The ra**ja Nell a**llowed to kiss her
(Through the **window**) chanced to miss her.

jeito   manner, way

Her open négli**gée too** plainly told
The secret of her **manner** brash and bold.

jura**r**   to swear

Do mea**sure Ar**thur's aptitude for lying:
Ask him **to swear** he's not afraid of dying!

lã   wool

Is it a ram, or is it a bull?
Lana will know when she shears the **wool**.

lábio   lip

You slob! the **lobby oo**zes muck and slime!
So button up your **lip** and put in time!

ladeira   slope

Lu**la, dare u**pon this **slope** to stand
And wave us onward to the Promised Land!

lado   side

Oo la **la! Do** fame and fortune hide?
I care not, if I have you by my **side**.

lago**s**ta   lobster

Beu**lah, ghost of** vanished years,
Salts her **lobster** with her tears.

lançar   to hurl, throw

You will not find **Lon sor**ry for his crimes.
He **hurls** the blame upon his life and times.

lápis (m.)   pencil

Sloppy son of sin, with hands prehensile,
Just keep your fingers off my silver **pencil**!

lata   can (n.)

—I find a **lotta** meat in what you say,
But just can't stand the way you prate and pray!
—So eat the meat and throw the **can** away!

leal   loyal

Lay our intrepid drummer on his bed.
Another **loyal** combatant is dead!

legar   to bequeath

Lay garden tools within the youngster's reach.
Bequeath him all the homely skills you teach.

lei (f.)   law

Lay down the **law**, sir, as you please.
But no one tells me when to sneeze!

leito   bed

He **lay too** still upon his **bed**.
I called his name: my friend was dead.

lento, -a   slow

Len too often seemed both **slow** and shy.
I shook his flabby hand and said goodbye.

le**r**   to read

I've **read** his thought: This man will dare
To beard the lion in his **lair**!

le**r**do, -a   clumsy, dull

B**lair**, **do** what you will and can
To help that charming, **clumsy** man!

letra   letter (alphabet), handwriting

The p**late Ra**mona tossed into the flames
Once bore the painted **letters** of our names.

leva**n**ta**r**   to raise, lift

Comrades, **lay von Tar**boldt slowly, sadly,
Before that altar which he **raised** so gladly.

leva**r**   to carry, take

I did p**lay var**sity, but now no more
Carry the ball or help to make a score.

leve   light (in weight)

Our medium looks so **light** in weight:
No doubt she's learned to **levi**tate.

liga**r** (1)   to bind, connect, join

Lee gardens all the spring and summer long,
And **binds** his tasks together with a song.

liga**r** (2)   to telephone

Lee garbles every tale he tells,
And when he **telephones**, he yells,
And so his project never jells.

ligeiro, -a   light, airy

Her né**gligée rou**tinely came undone.
A tale of love was **light** upon her tongue.

li**n**ha   streak, line, stripe

Ya cannot c<u>lea**n**, ya</u> just leave **streaks**,
And when ya go, the faucet leaks.

li**s**ta (1)   list (n.)

At **<u>least a</u>** dozen names are on the **list**:
The girls at school who never have been kissed.

li**s**ta (2)   stripe, strip (n.)

The tiger cannot change his **stripes**,
Nor **<u>Lee *s*to</u>**p airing ancient gripes.

livro   book

Just **<u>leave Ru</u>**th out of our wedding plans.
She wrote the **book** on also-rans!

lixo   trash, garbage

<u>Lee shoo</u>ed goats away from piles of **trash**.
(They ate the empty cans we sell for cash.)

logo   then

The agents of the **<u>law goo</u>**fed up again,
And **then** we knew they are not gods but men.

loucura   madness

It's **madness** how you waste your time exploring Aristotle
When our **<u>low Cura</u>**çao means you've got to buy a bottle!

louro, -a   blonde, golden

Blondes, I find, are mostly lazy.
Their s<u>low rou</u>tines just drive me crazy.

lua   moon

—And where were you this afternoon?
—I <u>flew a</u> mission to the **moon**.
—My friend, for me you're back too soon.

luga<i>r</i> (m.)   place (n.)

Lou <u>guar</u>ded her from every wrath and wrong,
And found a **place** to murmur love's old song.

luta<i>r</i>   to struggle, fight

Lou <u>tar</u>nished her bright image when, defeated,
She **struggled** half-way through the course—and cheated.

luva   glove

—I'll g<u>**lue Va**</u>nessa's **gloves** on. That way, they won't get lost.
—That's what you said the last time, so I'll keep my fingers
    crossed.

luxo   opulence, luxury

Lou <u>shoo</u>ts high. She hopes, at your expense,
To be a woman kept in **opulence**.

luz (f.)   light (n.)

Though b<u>luish</u> shadows blurred the **light**,
Our passion glowed throughout the night.

machuca*r*   to mash, bruise, crush

Ma, **shoo Car**los gently from our door,
Lest Pa should **mash** his ugly face once more!

madruga*r*   to get up early (in the morning)

When **Ma drew Gar**field out of bed, he swore
He'd never **get up early** any more.

magro, -a   thin, lean

When **Ma grew** just a little **thin**ner
We let her eat her birthday dinner.

maio*r*   larger, greater, older

My York's a busy English city,
Fast growing **larger**, more's the pity.

mai*s*   more

My sis annoys me with her giggling
And, even **more**, her chassis-wiggling.

mal   badly (adv.)

She hit him in the **mou**th. Her **badly** frightened lover
Was much too scared to pay her back. He simply took to cover.

mala   suitcase

M**oll o**ffended Pa. I gave her warning.
She'll have to pack her **suitcase** in the morning!

maluco, -a   mad, crazy

Ma, **Lu coo**s sweetly as a bird.
So is she **mad**, or just absurd?

mamar   to suckle

Ma**ma mar**ked (and how she chuckled!)
The slyness of the child she **suckled**.

man dar   to command, order

Hoot, **mon**! **Dar**win taught us to survive.
His law **commands**: Stay fit, and stay alive.

mão (f.)   hand

To **moun**t the stairs I offered her my **hand**—
A gesture that she failed to understand.

mar (m.)   sea, ocean

My goal it is to sail uncharted **seas**.
You shall not **mar** that dream with sophistries!

mas   but

My sister steers. I wonder where she's going?
I ask and ask, **but** still she just looks knowing.

mata   wood, forest

Ma, Tom opted for a good
Old-fashioned picnic in a **wood**,
Where kissing games are understood.

matar   to kill

Ma targeted a law degree,
But **killed** the scheme: it wasn't free!

mau, má   bad

What **bad mou**se has gnawed my cheese?
He didn't bother saying please.

| medo | fear (n.) |

May, do everything I ask you to.
And have no **fear**: I'll do the same for you.

| meio | half, middle, semi- |

May you prosper, may you laugh,
And all your pains be cut in **half**.

| melho*r* | better |

In Africa, **Mel, Yor**uba's the tongue
In which the **better** lullabies are sung.

| meno*r* | younger, smaller |

May Nora satisfy her hunger
For losing weight and looking **younger**!

| meno*s* | less |

May knew *S*ally was no fool,
But **less** than keen to go to school.

| me*n*tir | to lie (prevaricate) |

Me*n*, cheer*s* are sadly out of place.
Besides, you**'re lying** to my face.

| mê*s* (m.) | month |

In **May *S*amantha** went to France
To spend a **month** on pure romance.

| mesa | table |

May's a well-instructed cook.
She sets her **table** by the book.

mil   thousand

To **me you** wear a **thousand** faces,
Each with its own undreamed-of graces.

missa   Mass

To **me Sa**mantha seems a lass
Who stops for booze en route to **Mass**.

moço   boy

Though **Moe soo**n made the college girl give in,
The **boy** had found his patience wearing thin.

mole   tender, flabby, limp

Moe'll eat anything that's **tender**.
He doesn't ask about the gender!

mon*tan*ha   mountain

A deep **moan Tanya** uttered, turning blue,
Then stammered, "Get me quick some **Mountain** Dew!"

mora*r*   to live, reside

More artisans are needed for our city,
But only lawyers **live** here, more's the pity.

mor*n*o, -a   tepid, warm

More neutrality, and that less **tepid**,
Will help to make us pacifists intrepid.

morrer   to die

Ne**mo, hair** is not for tinting.
I'll **die** before I heed your hinting!

morte (f.)   death

With **more chi**canery than legal skill
Her **death** was plotted in her husband's will.

morto, –a   dead

The **more two** people come to bash and bore each other,
The more I say "Your love is **dead**. Go home to Mother!"

mos ca   fly (n.)

A lachry**mose ca**reer's ahead for that besotted
Young man who weeps for every moth and **fly** he's swatted.

mos trar   to show

Most rah-rah boys don't last too long,
And **show** small sense of right and wrong.

mun do   earth, world

Look at the **moon. Do** you know why
It follows the **earth** around the sky?

nada   nothing

Nod a while. Remember when you waken
There's **nothing** quite so good as eggs and bacon.

não   no, not

Now new leaders take the floor,
And **no**, they're not worth clapping for!

nariz (m.)   nose

Ma**n! a Rich**elieu could scarce expose
The plots that bloom beneath your very **nose**!

negar   to deny, refute

Nay, gardening is not enough,
Though few **deny** it keeps you tough.

nem   neither

The cops have got your **nam**e and license number,
And **neither**, you will grant, is useless lumber!

ninguém   no one, nobody

Ann, e'en games no more amuse us.
No one doubts they just confuse us.

noite (f.)   night

Don't an**noy Chi**huahuas in the **night**.
If you ignore their bark, you'll feel their bite.

nome (m.)   name

A **gnome e**merged, so drab and dumpy
'Twas no surprise his **name** was Grumpy.

nono, -a   ninth

No neurotic cat of mine
Shall lay his **ninth** life on the line
To chase your silly ball of twine.

notar   to note

Will all please **note**: This fag contains **no tar**!
It tastes and smokes just like a fine cigar!

nove   nine

I **gnaw vi**cuña steak, and in the end acknowledge
I never learned to cook in those **nine** years I spent in college.

noven ta   ninety

Gi**no, vent a** righteous rage
At orders barring from the stage
Actors **ninety** years of age.

nuca   nape (of neck)

A **new ca**tastrophe arose.
On the **nape** of my neck the small hairs froze:
The bears had eaten most of my clothes!

nun ca   never

At **noon Ka**tinka **never** ate a bite,
But she came home at five and gorged all night!

obra   work of art

I like to dr**aw Bra**zilian flowers and birds.
A **work of art** can tell you more than words!

ofer ta   offer

O fair Tallulah, take my **offer:**
Let me fill your hungry coffer!

olho   eye

Don't let troubles b**owl you** over.
Fix your **eye** on fields of clover.

on da   wave

My friend, Big-**Wave**-in-Ocean, wrote a
Book to prove he **own ed Da**kota.

ontem   yesterday

Joan tamed alone my passions wild.
When **yesterday** on me she smiled,
My heart forever was beguiled.

oprimir   to press, oppress

Why **press** me for the meaning of "pre-war"?
You surely kn**ow "pre" mere**ly means "before!"

ora   now, well (interj.)

Now, Ora thinks she has a mission
To solve our problems through nutrition.

orgulho   pride

Your **pride** is finding bones upon the plain,
For ghoul you are and ghoul you will remain.

ostra   oyster

My h**ost ro**bbed foreign clubs and cloisters
To serve his guests the finest **oysters**.

ou   or

Guy **owe**s either Bill **or** Ben a hundred dollars.
He'll pay it to the first of these two renegades who hollers.

ouro   gold

Oh, rule out the things that he did wrong.
Treasure the heart of **gold** you loved so long.

ousar   to dare

Oh, czars and kings and queens have loved this drink,
But what our Ma will say I **dare** not think!

outro, -a   other

Our nursery c**oatroo**m differs from all **others**,
For our small clients often bring their mothers.

ouvido   ear

O Vee, do listen when I try to scold you.
Have you no **ear** for all the things I've told you?

ouvir   to hear

Oh, virulent and just our indignation
At what we **hear** you've done to God's creation!

pagar   to pay

Pa, Garwood **pays** his doctor bills,
But just won't take those headache pills!

pai   father

—I'll cut a piece of **pie** for **Father**.
—He'll eat it whole, so please don't bother.

país   country (nation)

—**Pa, Eas**ter eggs now cost a buck, or near it.
—The **country** must be full of Easter spirit.

paladar (m.)   taste, palate (n.)

Poll, a darling girl with **taste**, supports
This dictum: "Share your pints, but not your quarts!"

pão (m.)   bread

The pontiff brought, with **bread**, a **pou**nd of butter.
"Infallible recipe!" I heard him mutter.

para   in order to, to

Pa robbed little Ernie's piggy-bank
In order to pursue some silly prank.

para**r**   to stop

Gas**par, ar**e you now a traffic cop?
I fear you've learned to go but not **to stop**!

parece**r**   to seem, appear

See **Pa race Sar**ah! Now, by gosh, he's caught 'er!
It **seems** this senior still outruns his daughter!

parede (f.)   wall

Pa, raging like a bull, upset us all
By smashing Mom's best plate against the **wall**!

par**tir**   to rend, crack, split

Gas**par, cheer**s and tears are all in vain.
You **rend** my heart, but cannot ease the pain.

passa**r**   to happen, pass

"What **happened**, Pa**pa**," Se**r**geant Poe demanded,
"To all those daring men you once commanded?"

pau (m.)   rod, stick

Ma **pou**nded on the table-top
With curtain-**rod** and kitchen mop:
"You bums! This wrangling's got to stop!"

paz (f.)   peace

Leave her in **peace**! Her "**spyish**" behavior
Was nothing more deadly than playing the clavier!

pedi*r*   to ask, ask for

Pay jeering crowds to go away.
And **ask** them not to spoil our day.

pedra   stone, pebble, rock

I'd **pay dra**matic prices for
A **stone** that marks the grave of war.

pega*r*   to seize, grasp

Pay Garth the modest sum you rashly promised him.
Then **seize** him, throw him in the creek. (He cannot swim.)

peito   chest, bosom, breast

You **pay too** much for medals which at best
Are tawdry ribbons for your manly **chest**.

peixe (m.)   fish

The **pay she** seeks, the job she wishes,
Elude her grasp like flies or **fishes**.

pela*r*   to peel off, remove

I won't **pay lar**ge amounts for stylish sunburn lotion.
I simply **peel** my clothes **off** fast and jump into the ocean.

pele (f.)   skin

A **pale, e**merging sun begins
To shed his pallor on our **skins**.

pena   torment, pain, suffering; sentence (law)

It was in **Spain A**rletta learned to suffer.
She found that **torments** only made her tougher.

pena**r**   to pain, distress, grieve

You don't **pain Ar**thur much when you shed tears.
But oh! your smiles **distress** him through the years!

pe*n*sa**r**   to think

I **think** a lecture on Old Irish art
Will surely o**pen Sar**ge O'Brien's heart.

pe*n*te (m.)   comb

In the **pen Chi**quita's **comb**
Is all they let her bring from home.

pequeno, -a   small, little (in size)

All of us **pay Kay new** compliments each day
Because she throws **small** smiles at us in that beguiling way.

pera   pear

Accept this knife; and, if you dare,
Use the same to **pare a pear**.

perceber   to perceive

"We do despair," say bears and jackals.
"You must perceive, from angry cackles,
Those cruel game laws raise our hackles!"

perder   to lose

This pair dare not try to live together.
They'd lose their time in fights about the weather—
Its when, its where, how long, how bad, and whether.

perdoar   to pardon

—That foul-mouthed pair do Arthur's meanest jobs.
—Oh, pardon them. They're just a brace of slobs!

perecer   to die, perish

You'll have to pay, Ray. Sara's daily wage
Is due until she dies from over-age.

perna   leg

The hard green pear Natasha hurled at me
Connected with my leg, and clipped my knee.

pertencer   to belong

A spare, tense aeronaut rose up and said,
"This girl belongs to me, alive or dead!"

pesar   to weigh

And who pays Arthurine to sing her song?
She weighs too much to charm me very long!

picar   to prick, sting

The hap**py car**load, munching Fritos,
Were **pricked** each moment by mosquitoes.

pintor   painter

Po**p, e'en tor**ture won't unlock the **painter**'s sullen lips.
He won't say why, for paint-brushes, he uses paper clips.

pior   worse

Peoria's an unexciting town,
And, **worse**, a butt of jokes to every clown.

piscar   to wink, blink

O hap**py scar**! It celebrates, I think,
The day sweet Iris taught me not to **wink**!

piscina   swimming pool

Has Hap**py seen a** fancy **swimming pool**?
If so, no garden hose will keep him cool.

pitada   pinch (of snuff, salt)

So, **Pete, odd** acquaintances of yours
Prefer a **pinch** of snuff to cans of Coors!

pó   dust

The **po**rtly fellow, crazed with lust,
Collapsed, despairing, in the **dust**.

poder   can, to be able

If we **could** find that mystic dell,
We'd see **Poe dar**ing heaven and hell
To find his long-lost Annabel.

poema (m.)   poem

Poe, aim a poem at Annabel.
She'll reply with a funeral knell.

po**r**   along, by, through

Pour the beer **along** the pier.
The girls will find you, never fear!

pô**r**   to set (table), place, put

Set the table, **pour** the wine,
Light the candles, ere we dine.

poré**m**   still, however

I'll just **pour Am**y's tasteless pudding out.
But **still**, the dog will eat it up, no doubt!

po**r** quê?   why? for what reason?

—**Pork** ably roasted makes your dinner easy.
—**Why** don't you serve it often? —It's too greasy.

po**r**que   because

Porky went to jail **because**
He feels a deep contempt for laws.
So who will spring him—Santa Claus?

po**r**ta   door

Dearest, into Tommy's coffee **pour**
Tabasco, then direct him to the **door**!

pouco, -a   few, small (in amount)

Poke cool ices down the victim's throat.
Ignore the **few** who stand around and gloat.

praga   scourge, plague

In **Prague a** tourist views a **scourge** of history.
Its future's dark; its past is veiled in mystery.

praia   beach

Pry Arturo out of bed
And send him to the **beach** instead.

precisa**r**   to need

Pray see czars torn off their thrones
And made to beg in humble tones
For coins they **need** for telephones.

preço   price

I **pray Su**sanna paid the **price**
For drinking gin and shooting dice.

prega**r**   to nail

Pray gardens will be many in our county,
And **nail** your hopes upon the summer's bounty.

premia**r**   to reward, give an award

With tears he'd s**pray me, ar**guing the while
That I **rewarded** gaiety with guile!

prender   to take, fasten, seize

Po**p, rend air**, and, if you must, say charms.
But **take** your errant daughter in your arms.

preso, -a   arrested (pp. of prender)

I **pray Zu**leika knows my aged knees are stiff and sore
From praying she'll try not to get **arrested** any more.

prestar   to lend, loan

Press Tarzan's pretty Jane to send us
The rhino hides she said she'd **lend** us.

preto, -a   dismal, black, dark

Pray to any faith you find enlightening
To help you think the **dismal** skies are brightening!

primor (m.)   exquisite beauty, artistry, delicacy

The Isle of Ca**pri mor**e than wine or wit
Speaks to my soul of **beauty exquisite**.

procurar   to seek, look for

I'm **pro-curar**e when I have **to seek**
Assassins down an Amazonian creek.

pronto, -a   alert, prepared, ready

Though lying **prone, too** stunned to be **alert**,
I saw how I had hit him where it hurt.

prosseguir   to proceed

You're a **pro, say gear** and garments.
Just **proceed**: you'll catch the varmints!

protela*r*   to postpone, delay

You're the **pro**. **Tell Ar**thur **to postpone**
His effort to produce a dial tone.

pula*r*   to jump, leap

Pool Arthur's wit with Jack's allusions.
You're sure **to jump** to false conclusions.

quadro   picture, square

The **squad drew** near and tried to case the joint.
They viewed the **picture**, but they missed the point.

qual   which (interrog. pro.)

—**Which** is the man who won the marathon?
—You saw our own Dic**k wow** the lookers-on.

qua*n*do   when

Sic**k, wa*n* Du**pré must face his final hour,
When law and order show at last their power.

qua*n*to   how much

—Dic**k, wa*n*t to** cultivate the golden touch?
—I guess I do. The question is, **How much?**

queima*r*   to burn, sear

Kay ma*r*velled at the lying and subversive things she heard,
But she had **burned** her bridges, so she didn't say a word.

que*m*   who (interrog.)

—**Who ca*m*e** today and woke us up so early?
—'Twas Pa, I'm sure, because the voice was surly.

querer   to like, love, want, wish

Though you s<u>care rare</u>ly, I should **like** to think
You might turn pale if this small boat should sink.

*r*apaz   boy, young man

My **boy**, if you d<u>rop pie sh</u>ells on the floor
You will not be invited anymore.

*r*ato   rat

T<u>rot, U</u>lrica, from your room.
That **rat** will drive you to your doom!

*r*eal   royal

Ray, <u>ou</u>st the rats that still infest our soil.
Our night life here has been a battle **royal**!

*r*ebela*r*   to revolt, rebel

—**Ray**, <u>bail Ar</u>thur out! He needs a jolting!
—He won't **revolt**, no matter how revolting!

*r*eclama*r*   to protest, complain

Let's go and <u>**rake Lamar**</u> across the coals!
The man **protests** his score each time he bowls!

*r*ecua*r*   to back away, recede, retreat

<u>**Ray**, **coo ar**</u>dently at Fanny May.
You'll find she just **backs** frostily **away**.

*r*ede (f.)   net, hammock

The <u>**rage E**</u>liza suffered when her brother won the bet
Was like the wrath of some great fish that flounders in the **net**.

reduzir   reduce, diminish, lessen

Ray, do zero in on young, impoverished girls,
Reduced to desperation, who have to sell their pearls!

rei   king

A **ray** of hope lights up the gloom.
The **King** has rented our front room!

reinado   reign

Rain ah! **doo**ms every native celebration
And brings a **reign** of gloom throughout the nation.

rematar   to end, close, finish

Ray, Ma targeted our school's decay.
She **ended** with a slap at PTA.

remeter (1)   to defer

Ray may terrorize the nation
If we **defer** his education.

remeter (2)   to send, deliver, remit

Ray may tear me quivering limb from limb
If I don't **send** that recipe to him.

requerer   to require, demand, request

Ray, Kay rarely will **require**
That you get up and start the fire.

resposta   response

The warrior headd**ress Paw s tu**ck on last night
Drew Mom's **response**: "You're spoiling for a fight!"

*r*etor*r*nar   to return, turn back (intr.)

Our country's suffered years of slash-and-burn.
At last the f**ray-torn ar**tists can **return**.

*r*ir   to laugh

—Servants' entrance in the **rear**?
—Sir, we all are servants here.
Praying, working, **laughing**, bored,
We monks are servants of the Lord.

*r*ocha   rock, crag

A hungry c**row sho**t down on yon high **rocks**,
To feast on Mama's bra and Dad's old socks.

*r*oda   wheel

We **rode a**long until we heard a squeal:
As usual, my car had lost a **wheel**.

*r*ogar   to pray, beg, plead

That **rogue Ar**thur snatched away my purse!
Come back, **I pray**, or dread your mother's curse!

*r*o*n*car   to snore

—What makes the old c**rone car**p and croak like that?
—She **snores** all night. Besides, her jokes fall flat.

*r*osto   face (n.)

A look mo**rose too** often seen
Darkened the **face** of England's Queen.

roubar   to rob

You must p**robe Ar**thur's links with crime.
He **robbed** his Ma of her last dime.

roupa   clothing

I'll **rope a** cow for leather **clothing**—
A job that fills my heart with loathing.

rua   street

The **true a**pproach to riches is through **streets**
Now trodden only by the world's elites.

saber   to know (a fact), know how to

Li**sa, bur**y false or useless knowledge,
Including some I **know** you got in college!

sacar   to take out (money)

Sock Arthur, grab his purse the way we planned,
And **take out** all the cash he has on hand.

saída   exit, departure

Of operas, Si**s, Aïda** is my favorite.
Let's linger at the **exit** here and savor it.

sair   to go out, leave

"El**sa," eer**ie voices utter,
"**Go out** and perish in the gutter!"

sal   salt

She dances like a **sow**. Her wit's at fault.
I guess she'll have to sit below the **salt**.

sala   hall, parlor

Sol, **a** lot of union members tell me
From our assembly **hall** you would expel me.

salpica**r**   to splash, spatter, sprinkle

See our **sow peek ar**dently at her up-beat new pen.
She hopes she'll soon be **splashing** us with gobs of mud again.

salsa   parsley

That old **souse** affects a **parsley** diet.
His friends approve, but won't consent to try it.

se   if

If she **see**s forbidden fruit,
She eats it up—she thinks it's cute.

seca**r**   to dry

Say, **Car**l, do arbitrate this wrangle.
Good sense **dries** up when lovers tangle!

século   century

You won't, in half a **sec**, **cool Lu**ke's desire to marry you.
For half a **century**, at least, the guy will harry you!

sede (f.)   thirst, craving, desire

I **say Jea**n Ann has an unbounded **thirst**
For knowledge of the best and of the worst!

segui**r**   to follow

Say ghee repels. It **follows**, as the night the day,
You'll never learn to cook your food the Indian way.

seio   breast, bosom

I do not **say you** actually stink.
What oozes from your **breast** is printer's ink.

se**m**   without

It's not the **same without** you, dear.
For once, my bank account is clear.

semana   week

The boys **say Ma kno**cked out a thug or two.
Next **week** she may be practicing on YOU!

se**n**ta**r**   to seat

The general **sent Ar**my troops to save us
And barber chairs in which **to seat** and shave us.

se**n**ti**r**   to feel, be sorry, regret

The winning goal **sent cheer**s to every tongue.
That day we **felt** we were forever young.

se**r**   to be (held)

A **cer**emony **will be** held at seven
To celebrate our child's new life in Heaven.

si**m**   yes

—**Yes**, you **seem** a silly lout.
Do you know what the war's about?
—Does anybody? That I doubt.

sinal (m.)   signal; traffic light

I've not **seen ou**t the window since I gave
A **signal** that I'd gladly be your slave.

só   only, alone, sole

I **only sought** a little peace and quiet.
How can you think I'd try to start a riot?

sobra   excess, remainder

The muffled threats got louder. In the press
We **saw bra**vado swell into **excess**.

sobre   upon, on

I'm **so Bri**tannic in my every taste
The Union Jack's tattooed **upon** my waist.

sol (m.)   sun

Her **sou**l is like the winter **sun**:
It sheds no glow on anyone.

soltar   to unloose, release

So target, dear, his middle-aged affection,
And he'll **unloose** his cash without objection.

somar   to add

So marvelous it seems to me
My child can **add** thirteen and three—
I wonder what the sum can be!

sonhador   dreamer

Sonya, **door**s will open to the **dreamer**
Who dares to tame a wallaby or lemur!

sonhar   to dream

Pepys' **own yar**n describes how Britain fared
When church and state together **dreamed** and dared.

sono   sleep (n.)

So neurotic is this creep
He plays the market in his **sleep**.

sorri*r*   to smile

So hea*r* me out and **smile**. But let me mention
That all I really wanted was a pension.

so*r*te (f.)   luck

Her **so*r*e chi**huahua bit my heel.
It's just my **luck**. There's no appeal.

sossega*r*   to calm

—**So, say gar**lands deck my door!
I still find Christmas just a bore!
—Friend, **calm** yourself and say no more.

subi*r*   to climb, go up, mount

Sue, bee*r* won't help you **climb** that peak
Or reach more distant goals you seek.

súbito   suddenly

I counselled **Sue, "Be to**mblike and oblivious
To Bernard's glance so **suddenly** lascivious."

suco   juice

—Why doesn't **Sue cool** off? —She's too obtuse
To settle for some home-made orange **juice**!

sul (m.)   south

I'll **sue** my wife for all her wealth.
She took my child down **south** by stealth.

superar   to surpass; overcome

Super-arguments like yours
Surpass the spiels for guided tours.

supor   to suppose, presume

Sue poured hot soup in Grandpa's nose—
A fate he's used to, I **suppose**.

tal   such

I'll **tout** some stocks, but never **such**
As pay too little, cost too much.

tanto   so much

That débu**tante too** often drinks
So much she tells you what she thinks!

tão   so (adv.)

I am **so** young that when we drive to **town**
I feel both heart and tongue jump up and down.

tarde (f.) (1)   afternoon

This **afternoon** we'll catch the show,
And cheer its s**tar, Je**ronimo.

tarde (2)   late (adv.)

We thought we'd s**tar Je**an Ann in that new drama,
But learned too **late** she'll soon become a mama.

tem   there is, there are

There's fear we'll never lose the **tain**t
Of seeing things the way they ain't.

temer   to fear

S<u>tay mer</u>ry while the Christmas feast continues,
Though drink, I **fear**, is rotting out our sinews!

temor (m.)   fear, dread (noun)

<u>Tame or</u>dinary birds and make them talk.
No **fear** that people will not stand and gawk!

tempo (1)   time

S<u>tem poo</u>r Sadie's urge to rhyme.
Her jingles are a waste of **time**.

tempo (2)   weather

—S<u>tem poo</u>r Annie's plaints about the **weather**.
—It matters little, since we're all together.

ter   to hold, have, possess

By **<u>ter</u>**ror **held**, the robber, once so bold,
Now shook with fear, and dropped his sacks of gold.

terceiro   third (n.)

—And did the daf**<u>t heir say ru</u>**de things to you?
—Yes, but at least a **third** of them are true.

ternura   tenderness

<u>Tear neura</u>sthenic moods from troubled Bess,
And treat her firmly but with **tenderness**.

testa   forehead

—What carved those furrows in your **forehead**?
—A **<u>test o</u>**ccurred, and it was horrid!

tirar   to take away, take off, take out

Cheer Arthur with your fiddle. **Take away**
The problems he has wrestled with all day.

tocar (1)   to touch

Ot**to, car**t your guns away.
Gravely **touch** your heart and say
From this moment you will do
Everything I ask you to.

tocar (2)   to play (a musical instrument)

I met Joe Bar**tow car**ting home a banjo.
I sneered and muttered, "**Play** it if you can, Joe!"

todo, -a   every, all

—I cut my **toe. Do** see how **every** vein is bleeding!
—I'll fix it, though I'd rather go on reading!

tomar   to take, drink, eat

Bere**ft, O Mar**garet, of your affections,
I'll **take** a chance on other predilections,
Like carving traitors into small, neat sections!

topar   to bump (into), butt, come upon

S**tow par**t of the booty in bra and pants,
And try not **to bump** into maiden aunts!

tossir   to cough

S**tow ser**ious remembered wrongs away.
The thieves may **cough** your money up some day!

traçar   to trace

The Con**tra ser**geant couldn't **trace**
That dark, elusive Indian face.

tragar   to swallow

We'll send an ex**tra guar**d to Sleepy Hollow,
Though Rip van Winkle's yarn is hard **to swallow**.

tratar   to treat

Trot artists out and let them **treat** of painting,
At least until we're at the point of fainting.

trazer   to bring

Ex**tras air** their talents on the beach,
Bringing tips and gossip each to each.

treinar   to train, drill

You must **train Ar**thur not to smoke or eat
While **training** for the chimney-sweepers' meet.

tremer   to tremble, shudder

It's just a fact: **Ray mer**its this disgrace,
And yet I **tremble** when I see his face!

tremor (m.)   quiver, shiver, thrill, tremor (n.)

Your en**trée more** than satisfied our highest expectations.
I feel a **quiver**, though. I fear digestive complications.

trocar   to exchange, barter, change, transform

Maes**tro Car**lo just **exchanged** his life
Of bachelor boredom for domestic strife.

último, -a   last

Shoes by **Gucci mo**ve the feet
Of these, the **last** of our elite.

um, uma   one, a, an

Boo**m**er, **one** time every year
Forgets himself and sheds a tear.

uni**r**   to unite, join

Too far we are to re**unite**,
Too near to try to end our fight,
Too stupid, both, to set things right!

u**n**ta**r**   to daub, spread

Soo**n Tar**zan will come swinging on the breeze,
Daubing his private mark on all the trees.

usa**r**   to wear, use

Do you **wear** Army issue clothes? Attention!
Lose Army garments and you lose your pension!

uva   grape

You've arrived in time for **grapes** and cheese.
And have you further needs? We strive to please.

vaca   cow

Pro**voca**tive to every **cow** is Ferdinand the bull.
They know they owe a lot to him who keeps their udders full.

vareta   switch, slender stick

Our teachers, **Eva, rate a** straight A plus:
They never even used a **switch** on us!

velho, -a   old

This fine **old** cara**vel you** used to sail
Is still so stout it weathers every gale.

ve**n**de**r**   to sell

S**ven** da**re**d **to sell** his Olga's sable
To put some meat upon the table.

ve**n**to   wind

S**ven, to** Jane, has never sinned.
To me he's just a bag of **wind**!

ve**r**   to see

Verily the truth has come to me:
None are so blind as those who will not **see**.

ve**s**ti**r**   to clothe, dress

—Your red **ves**t **cheer**s me when I'm weary.
—It could not **clothe** a heart more dreary.

vi**r**   to come

Virulence is always useful
For those who **come** to us excuseful.

visita   visit

Har**vey's eata**bility, it seems,
To my pet vulture is the stuff of dreams.
That's why his **visits** here are marked by screams!

viver   to live, be alive

Da**vy ver**y often gives
A false report on how he **lives**.
He spends each work-day making sieves.

volta   turn, return (n.)

The fateful **turn** in that lost **vote o**ccurred
When our great leader broke his sacred word.

volta**r**   to come back, return (intr.)

The last **vote ar**med us with the right
To come back here by day or night.

FINAL EXAMINATION

Each of the 50 jingles below contains the sounds of a Portuguese word that you have learned from this book. The jingles themselves you have not seen before. They are constructed just like those in the text. Find and underscore the consecutive syllables that approximate the sound of the Portuguese word.

When you have finished the test, turn to page 78 and check your answers. If your answers are all correct, you can congratulate yourself on a not inconsiderable achievement.

1. The happy scene around your **swimming pool**
    Is like our lovely hostess—calm and cool.

2. Roving scholars, drawn by curiosity,
    Called our school's new **wing** a sheer monstrosity.

3. Moll, you feed on **garlic**, catfood, worms.
    Whoever sees such self-indulgence squirms!

4. He very often managed **to be seen**
    Dancing attendance on the Campus Queen.

5. Tyrant, you have shut the door on reason.
    May **pain** pursue you in and out of season!

6. In the hospital I drank a liter of the stuff.
    The doctor **there** forgot to say a teaspoon was enough!

7. Ah, Lou, new **students** always seem to find
   Our school's a splendid place to rest the mind.

8. I paid Ramona fifty cents
   To throw no **stones** at my front fence!

9. Now roar a while, O dragon, but don't be too insistent,
   For since the **dawn** of common sense we've known you're
       non-existent!

10. You broke our party into factions.
    The town won't tolerate **such** actions!

11. In fabled Oz a tale I heard him sing—
    A snow-white sea-bird with a broken **wing**.

12. —Say, does Eva rate a date with Jim?
    —If he says No, I'll take a **switch** to him!

13. O Paul Revere, light lamps for me,
    One if by land, two if by sea.
    You'll **come** by air? Resort to three!

14. Moll abides by just one rule:
    When you're lost in Istanbul,
    Grip your **suitcase**, keep your cool!

15. —Your love, the Bey, must treat you rather **well**.
    —He opened up the gates of Heaven and Hell!

16. A true assertion may be indiscreet,
    So don't proclaim your doctrines in the **street**!

17. So mark my words, and, maybe, since it's you,
    From time to time I'll let you **add** a few.

18. Coe, heed a warning ere you raise your banners.
    I fear you'll never win a **race** for manners.

19. Though bruised and sore, Chiquita had the **luck**
    To shoot the villain ere the man could duck.

20. Some plaintive Scottish lays the wandering minstrels sang
    Until some just-invented **law** declared the troupe a gang!

21. In town new comrades let me know
    What makes the people hate me **so**.

22. Should I keep my **mouth** shut? I hate to cause you pain,
    But I just saw your latest beau cavorting with Elaine.

23. She will not pay, she slithers like a **fish**
    That makes its silent exit with a swish.

24. Do take a day, Ramona, to think before you marry.
    Just find a **seat** and brood all night if you're considering
    Harry!

25. That Inca lords it over the tribe,
    But rouses **heat** when he won't imbibe.

26. Ma simply wouldn't eat the food I had.
    Her after-Christmas appetite was **bad**.

27. Duncan ate a meal, and paid again
    With half a dozen scratches of his **pen**.

28. In a garden Sue will not **deny** you
    Unless her rival's set herself to buy you.

29. The mailman's cart arrived, weighed down with **letters**
    Dispatched to us by indigent go-getters
    Who hope to live on handouts from their betters.

30. The local people all say Bo lamented
    The scent of **onions** on the farm he rented.

31. Yes, Kay, ceremony has its place.
    But don't **forget**: he slapped you in the face!

32. Train artists to enhance their painting skills,
    And **train** them, too, to draw up valid wills.

33. Pray Susan won't disdain my beans and rice.
    For as to steak, I can't afford the **price**.

34. Men, say a prayer before you start your **suppers**
    That this raw steak won't make you lose your uppers.

35. To me Samantha is a saint.
    She goes to **Mass**, she wears no paint.
    If I should kiss her, would she faint?

36. A **hundred** times we've heard the same old tale:
    You got in trouble and you can't make bail.

37. Little Sue coos softly to induce
    Her grandma to bring on the orange **juice**.

38. Beside your rustic well you barbecue a **rabbit**.
    And that, my dear, is why I've made your table such a habit.

39. Ma grew **thinner** when she tried
    Diet pills and cyanide.
    Which works better? You decide.

40. Herman's prone to say whatever Herman thinks.
    Alert to do the same, I'll swear that Herman stinks.

41. —What happened, Bess, to cloud your pretty **forehead**?
    —An English test, a thing that's simply horrid!

42. You cheat on me **without** the slightest shame
Because you know I'll love you just the same.

43. Pow! he fell, struck by a sturdy **rod**
Wielded by his own tempestuous god.

44. The crew devoured their dogfish **raw**.
But oh! it stuck in Caleb's craw!

45. Today Fay reared a column to **approve**
The people she considers "in the groove."

46. The day she made that legendary feast,
Jen garnered **ten** proposals at the least.

47. Lon, Sartre **hurled** the javelin of thought
Against a world halfway to madness wrought.

48. Chagall, you gave us **branches** red and gold
To typify the grace of growing old.

49. So neurotic are your youthful crimes,
Your very **sleep** pollutes our life and times.

50. —Are you jumpy, or depressed?
—Whichever's **worse**. —I might have guessed.

ANSWERS TO
FINAL EXAMINATION

1. hap**py scene** around
2. sch**olars**
3. M**oll, you**
4. ve*r*y
5. doo*r*
6. a liter
7. **Ah, Lou, new**
8. **paid Ra**mona
9. Now **roar a**
10. **tow**n
11. **Oz a**
12. **Eva rate a**
13. Reve*re*
14. **Moll** abides
15. **Bey,** *m*ust
16. t*r*ue assertion
17. so, ma*r*k
18. **Coe, heed a**
19. so*re*, **Chi**quita
20. pl**ai**ntive
21. **tow***n*
22. **beau ca**vorting
23. **pay, she**
24. take **a day, Ra**mona
25. In**ca lo***r*ds

26. **Ma w**ouldn't
27. Dun**can ate a**
28. In **a ga***r*den
29. **ca***rt* arrived
30. **say Bo la**mented
31. Y**e***s*, **Kay, ce***r*emony
32. **Train a***r*tists
33. **Pray Su**san
34. **say a**
35. **me Sa**mantha
36. sa*me*
37. **Sue coo***s*
38. rustic **well you**
39. **Ma grew**
40. **prone to**
41. t**e***st*, **a**
42. sa*me*
43. **Pow**!
44. **crew**
45. To**day Fay rea***r*ed
46. **day she**
47. **Lo***n*, **Sa***r*tre
48. Cha**gall, you**
49. **So neu**rotic
50. jum**py, o***r*

APPENDIX
Guide to Pronunciation

This section is included in case you would like a brief view of the basic rules of Carioca Portuguese pronunciation.

VOWELS * AND DIPHTHONGS

Portuguese	*English Approximation*
a	a in father
a	a before s or z in a stressed word-final syllable is pronounced like the i in ice
ã	Lana, but even more nasalized
ai	ice
ãe	i in mine, but even more nasalized
au	cow
ão	clown, but even more nasalized
am (when word-final)	clown, but even more nasalized
am/an	come (when am or an ends a syllable that does not end a word)
e (when word-final)	me
e, ê	gate
é (sometimes e)	bed
ei	they
eu	they went
em/en (when syllable-final)	paint, but even more nasalized

Portuguese	*English Approximation*
i	greet
im/in (when syllable-finál)	mean, but even more nasalized
o, ô, ou	note
o (when word-final)	moo
o	before s or z in a stressed word-final syllable the o is pronounced like oy in boy
ó (sometimes o)	caught
oi	boy
õe	oink
om/on (when syllable-final)	own
u	loop
u	before s or z in a stressed word-final syllable the u is pronounced like we
ua	water
ui	we
um/un (when syllable-final)	raccoon

* A vowel carrying a diacritical mark (´ ` ~ ^) is always stressed.

CONSONANTS

b	banana
c (before a, o, u)	cart
c (before e and i)	seem
ç	saw
ch	shirt
d	dough
di	jeep
de (when word-final or alone)	jeep

Portuguese	*English Approximation*
f	farm
g (before a̱, o̱, u̱)	g̱oal
g (before e̱, i̱)	beig̱e
h	ẖ is silent
j	beig̱e
l (when syllable-initial)	little
l (when syllable-final)	Peru̱
lh	milli̱on
m (when syllable-initial)	ma̱ma̱
m (when syllable-final)	m̱ is silent and preceding vowel is nasalized (see Convention 1, page xi). In this book, this m̱ is in bold italics (***m***).
n (when syllable-initial)	ṉet
n (when syllable-final)	ṉ is silent and preceding vowel is nasalized (see Convention 1, page xi). In this book, this ṉ is in bold italics (***n***).
nh	y̱es. The ṉ is silent and a vowel that precedes it is nasalized
p	sp̱y̱
qu (before a̱, o)	q̱uality
qu (before e̱, i̱)	ḵey
r	potṯy (see Convention 2, page xii)
r	ẖunk (see Convention 2, page xii). In this book, this ṟ is in bold italics (***r***).
rr	highly exaggerated ẖ approximating the j̱ in Spanish
s (between vowels)	oozi̱ng
s (before voiced consonants)	beig̱e, raj̱

Portuguese	English Approximation
s (before unvoiced consonants)	shirt, also sh in word-final position (see Convention 3, pages xii – xiii). In this book, this s is in bold italics (*s*).
ss	sap
t	tot
ti	cheese
te (when word-final or alone)	cheese
v	victory
x	shirt
x (ex + vowel)	zebra
x (ex + consonant)	estrogen
x	in a few words x is pronounced like the x in axe
x	in few words x is pronounced like the s in sap
z	zebra
z (when word-final)	shirt in word-final position

GLOSSARY

English	Portuguese
a	um
able, be	poder
accept	aceitar
ache (v.)	doer
act (n.)	ato
add	somar
afternoon	tarde (1)
against	contra
agricultural	agrícola
air (n.)	ar
airy	ligeiro
alert	pronto
alive, be	viver
all	todo
alone	só
along	por
aloof	arisco
although	embora
among	entre
an	um
ancestry	estirpe
and	e
anger	cólera
animal (any unspecified)	bicho
answer (telephone) (v.)	atender

English	Portuguese
ant	formiga
appear	parecer
approve	deferir
arrested (adj.)	preso
arrive	chegar
artistry	primor
as	como
ask (for)	pedir
assail	arremeter
at	em
attack (v.)	arremeter
attend	assistir
attentive, be	atender
avoid	esquivar, evitar
back away	recuar
bad	mau
badly	mal
ball	bola
bank note	cédula
bar (law)	foro
barter	trocar
base (v.)	fundar
be (held)	ser
be (temporarily)	estar
beach	praia
beacon	farol
beard	barba
beastie	bicho
beautiful	belo
because	porque
bed	cama, leito
beg	rogar
believe	achar
belligerent	bélico
belly	barriga

English	*Portuguese*
belong	pertencer
bequeath	legar
better	melhor
between	entre
beyond (adv.)	além
big	grande
bind	ligar (1)
bishop	bispo
black	preto
blink	piscar
blonde	louro
body	corpo
book	livro
bosom	peito, seio
both	ambos
boy	moço, rapaz
brake (v.)	frear
branch	galho
bread	pão
breast	peito, seio
breeze	brisa
brim	beira
bring	buscar, trazer
brother	irmão
bruise (v.)	machucar
bud (v.)	brotar
build	construir
bump (into)	topar
burn	abrasar, arder, queimar
but	mas
butchershop	açougue
butt (v.)	topar
by	por
call (v.)	chamar
calm (v.)	sossegar

English	Portuguese
can (n.)	lata
can (v.)	poder
cargo	carga
carry	levar
cat	gato
caw (n.)	grasnada
cease	cessar
century	século
chair	cadeira
chamber	câmara
change (v.)	trocar
cheap	barato
chest (anat.)	peito
chicken	frango
choke	abafar
cinnamon	canela
city	cidade
class	aula
clever	esperto
climb	escalar, subir
close	rematar
clothe (v.)	vestir
clothing	roupa
clumsy	lerdo
coast	costa
cock	galo
comb	pente
come	vir
come back	voltar
come to blows	brigar
come upon	topar
command (v.)	mandar
commit	cometer
complain	reclamar
conceal	esconder

English	*Portuguese*
connect	ligar (1)
contained in, be	caber
cough (v.)	tossir
countenance	figura
country (nation)	país
course	aula
cow	vaca
crack (v.)	partir
crag	rocha
craving	sede
crazy	maluco
crisis	crise
croak (n.)	grasnada
cross	cruz
crude	cru
cruise (v.)	cruzar
crush (v.)	amassar, machucar
crying (n.)	choro
curb (v.)	frear
cursed	danado
cut (v.)	cortar
damned	danado
dance (v.)	dançar
dare	ousar
dark	preto
daub (v.)	untar
dawn	aurora
day	dia
dead	morto
dear	caro
death	morte
decree (n.)	cédula
defense	defesa
defer	remeter (1)
delay	protelar

English	*Portuguese*
delicacy	primor
delicious	gostoso
deliver	remeter (2)
demand (v.)	requerer
deny	negar
departure	saída
desire	sede
dial (telephone) (v.)	discar
die	morrer, perecer
diminish	reduzir
dismal	preto
distress (v.)	penar
door	porta
doubt (v.)	duvidar
drag (v.)	arrastar
dread (n.)	temor
dream (v.)	sonhar
dreamer	sonhador
dress (v.)	vestir
drill (v.)	treinar
drink (n.)	bebida
drink (v.)	beber, tomar
drop (n.)	gota
dry (v.)	secar
dull	lerdo
dust	pó
each	cada
ear	ouvido
early	cedo
earth	mundo
eat	comer, tomar
edge	beira
effort	esforço
embrace (n.)	abraço
end (n.)	fim

English	*Portuguese*
end (v.)	rematar
endeavor	esforço
enjoy	gostar
enough, be	bastar
epoch	época
equal (adj.)	igual
every	todo
examine	averiguar
excess	sobra
exchange (v.)	trocar
exit (n.)	saída
expect	esperar
expensive	caro
exquisite beauty	primor
extend	estender
extol	gabar
eye	olho
face (n.)	cara, rosto
"face"	careta
fact	fato
fair	belo
farewell	adeus
fasten	prender
father	pai
fear (n.)	medo, temor
fear (v.)	temer
feed (v.)	alimentar
feel	sentir
feel pain	doer
fertilizer	adubo
fetch	buscar
few (pron.)	pouco
fight (v.)	lutar, brigar
figure (n.)	figura
find	achar

English	*Portuguese*
find out	apurar (1)
fine (adv.)	bem
finger	dedo
finish	rematar
fish	peixe
fit into	caber
flabby	mole
floor (story; of a building)	andar
flower	flor
fly (n.)	mosca
fog	bruma
follow	seguir
food	alimento
for what reason?	por quê
force (n.)	força
forehead	testa
forest	mata
forget	esquecer
fork	garfo
forum	foro
found	fundar
friend	amigo
frighten	assustar
from	de
fruit	fruta
fry	fritar
full	farto
furnace	forno
gallantry	garbo
garbage	lixo
garlic	alho
get	buscar
get up early (in the morning)	madrugar
give	dar
give an award	premiar

English	Portuguese
give the date of	datar
glove	luva
glutted	farto
go	ir
go out	sair
go up	subir
gold	ouro
golden	louro
good	bom
grace	garbo
grandfather	avô
grandmother	avó
grant (v.)	deferir
grape	uva
grasp (v.)	pegar
great	grande
greater	maior
grieve (v.)	penar
grimace	careta
grow	crescer
guide (n.)	guia
gun	arma
half	meio
hall	sala
hammock	rede
hand	mão
handwriting	letra
happen	passar
happy	alegre
have (aux.)	haver, ter
he	ele
head	cabeça
headlight	farol
hear	ouvir
heat (n.)	calor

English	*Portuguese*
heed	atender
hence	daí
here	aqui, cá
hide	esconder
high	alto
hillbilly	caipira
hit (v.)	chocar
hit upon	acertar
hold	ter
hope (n.)	esperança
hope (v.)	esperar
hour	hora
house	casa
how	como
how much	quanto
however	porém
hug (n.)	abraço
hundred	cem
hurl	lançar
if	se
in	em
in order to	para
index card	ficha
inhale	aspirar
inquire	averiguar
insect (any unspecified)	bicho
instruction	ensino
island	ilha
isle	ilha
join	ligar (1), unir
juice	suco
jump	pular
jungle	floresta
keep	guardar
kill	matar

English	*Portuguese*
king	rei
kiss (n.)	beijo
know (a fact)	saber
know how to	saber
lady	dona
larger	maior
last	último
late (adv.)	tarde (2)
laugh (v.)	rir
law	lei
lay	deitar
lean	magro
leap (v.)	pular
learn	aprender
leave	sair
leg	perna
lend	prestar
less	menos
lessen	reduzir
letter	carta
letter (alphabet)	letra
lie (prevaricate)	mentir
lift	levantar
light (n.)	luz
light (airy)	ligeiro
light (in weight)	leve
like (adv.)	como
like (v.)	gostar, querer
limp (adj.)	mole
line	linha
lineage	estirpe
lip	beira, lábio
list (n.)	lista (1)
little (in size)	pequeno
live	viver

English	Portuguese
live (reside)	morar
load (n.)	carga
loan (v.)	prestar
lobster	lagosta
look for	procurar
lose	perder
love (n.)	amor, carinho
love (v.)	amar, querer
loyal	leal
luck	sorte
lunch	almoço
luxury	luxo
mad	maluco
madness	loucura
man	homem
manner	jeito
manure	adubo
mash (v.)	machucar
Mass	missa
master (n.)	amo
meat	carne
meat market	açougue
merry	alegre
middle	meio
mist	bruma
month	mês
moon	lua
moor (v.)	amarrar
more	mais
mount (v.)	subir
mountain	montanha
mouth	boca
nail (v.)	pregar
name (n.)	nome
nape (of neck)	nuca

English	*Portuguese*
need (v.)	precisar
neglect (v.)	descuidar
neither	nem
net	rede
never	nunca
night	noite
nine	nove
ninety	noventa
ninth	nono
no	não
no one	ninguém
nobody	ninguém
nose	nariz
not	não
note (v.)	notar
notebook	caderno
nothing	nada
now (interj.)	ora
ocean	mar
of	de
offer (n.)	oferta
old	velho
older	maior
on	em, sobre
one	um
onion	cebola
only	só
open (v.)	abrir
oppress	oprimir
opulence	luxo
or	ou
order (v.)	mandar
other	outro
ought	dever
outside	fora

English	*Portuguese*
oven	forno
over there	além
overcome	superar
overlook	descuidar
owe	dever
ox	boi
oyster	ostra
pain (n.)	dor, pena
pain (v.)	penar
painter	pintor
palate	paladar
pardon (v.)	perdoar
parlor	sala
parsley	salsa
party	festa
pass (v.)	passar
pay (v.)	pagar
peace	paz
peak	cima
pear	pera
pebble	pedra
peel off (v.)	pelar
pen	caneta
pencil	lápis
perceive	perceber
perfect (v.)	apurar (2)
perish	perecer
permit (n.)	cédula
picture	quadro
pinch (of snuff, salt)	pitada
place (n.)	lugar
place (v.)	colocar, pôr
plague	praga
play (musical instrument)	tocar (2)
plead	rogar

English	*Portuguese*
poem	poema
possess	ter
postpone	adiar, protelar
pound (v.)	amassar
praise (v.)	gabar
pray	rogar
prepared	pronto
present (adj.)	atual
presume	supor
press	oprimir
price	preço
prick	picar
pride	orgulho
proceed	prosseguir
protest (v.)	reclamar
put	colocar, pôr
quack (n.)	grasnada
quiver (n.)	tremor
rabbit	coelho
race (n.)	corrida
rain (v.)	chover
raise	levantar
rat	rato
raw	cru
read	ler
ready	pronto
rebel (v.)	rebelar
recede	recuar
reduce	reduzir
refute	negar
regret (v.)	sentir
reign (n.)	reinado
release (v.)	soltar
remain	ficar
remainder	sobra

English	*Portuguese*
remit	remeter (2)
remove	pelar
rend	partir
request (v.)	requerer
require	requerer
reside	morar
response	resposta
restrain	frear
retreat (v.)	recuar
return (n.)	volta
return (v. intr.)	retornar, voltar
revolt (v.)	rebelar
reward (v.)	premiar
ribbon	fita
rice	arroz
rim	beira
road	caminho
rob	roubar
rock (n.)	pedra, rocha
rod	pau
room	câmara
rooster	galo
rouse	comover
royal	real
salt	sal
same	igual
sand	areia
savory	gostoso
say	dizer
scale (v.)	escalar
scene	cena
school	escola
scourge	praga
scream (v.)	gritar
sea	mar

English	*Portuguese*
sear	queimar
search (n.)	busca
search (v.)	catar
seat (n.)	cadeira
seat (v.)	sentar
see	ver
seek	procurar
seem	parecer
seize	pegar, prender
sell	vender
sell on credit	fiar (1)
semi-	meio
send	remeter (2)
sentence (law)	pena
set (v.)	pôr
set fire to	acender
shape (n.)	figura
she	ela
shiver (n.)	tremor
shock (v.)	chocar
shore	costa
shout (v.)	gritar
show (v.)	mostrar
shudder (v.)	tremer
shun	esquivar, evitar
side (n.)	lado
signal	sinal
sing	cantar
skin	pele
slaughterhouse	açougue
sleep (n.)	sono
sleep (v.)	dormir
slender stick	vareta
slope	ladeira
slow (adj.)	lento

English	*Portuguese*
small (in amount)	pouco
small (in size)	pequeno
smaller	menor
smash into	chocar
smile (v.)	sorrir
smother	abafar
snore	roncar
so	assim, tão
so much	tanto
sobbing (n.)	choro
soccer	futebol
sole (adj.)	só
some	algum
son	filho
sorry, be	sentir
soul	alma
south	sul
spatter	salpicar
speak	falar
sphere	esfera
splash (v.)	salpicar
split (v.)	partir
spread (v.)	untar
sprinkle (v.)	salpicar
square (n.)	quadro
squeeze (v.)	apertar
staff (team)	equipe
stage (n.)	cena
star	estrela
steer (n.)	boi
stick	pau
stifle (v.)	abafar
still	ainda, porém
sting (v.)	picar
stock (n.)	estirpe

English	Portuguese
stomach	barriga
stone (n.)	pedra
stop (v.)	parar
story (of a building)	andar
streak (n.)	linha
street	rua
stretch out	estender
strip (n.)	lista (2)
stripe	linha, lista (2)
struggle (v.)	lutar
student	aluno
subdue	domar
such	tal
suckle	mamar
suddenly	súbito
suffer	doer
suffering	dor, pena
sugar	açúcar
suitcase	mala
summit	cima
sun	sol
supper	ceia
suppose	supor
sure	certo
surly	arisco
surpass	superar
suspicious	arisco
swallow (v.)	tragar
swear	jurar
sweet	doce
swimming pool	piscina
switch	vareta
table	mesa
take	levar, prender, tomar
take away	tirar

English	*Portuguese*
take off	tirar
take out	tirar
take out (money)	sacar
talk (v.)	falar
tall	alto
tame (v.)	domar
tape	fita
taste (n.)	paladar
tasty	gostoso
tea	chá
teach	ensinar
team (staff)	equipe
telephone (v.)	ligar (2)
tell	dizer
ten	dez
tender (adj.)	mole
tenderness	ternura
tepid	morno
that (over yonder)	aquele
that (near listener)	esse
that (just mentioned)	esse
that (previously mentioned)	aquele
then	então, logo
thence	daí
there	aí, ali
there are	tem
there is	tem
thin	magro
thing	coisa
think	achar, pensar
third	terceiro
thirst (n.)	sede
this (adj.)	este
though	embora
thousand	mil

English	*Portuguese*
thrill (n.)	tremor
through	por
throw (v.)	lançar
thus	assim
tie (v.)	atar
tie up (v.)	amarrar, atar
time	época, tempo (1)
tire (v.)	cansar
to	para
toe	dedo
token	ficha
torment (n.)	pena
touch (v.)	tocar (1)
trace (v.)	traçar
traffic light	sinal
train (v.)	treinar
training	ensino
transform	trocar
trash	lixo
treat (v.)	tratar
tremble (v.)	tremer
tremor (n.)	tremor
turn (n.)	volta
turn back	retornar
turn off (lights, stove)	apagar
turn on	acender
understand	entender
unfasten	desligar
unglue	descolar
unite	unir
unloose	soltar, desligar
until	até
upon	sobre
use (v.)	usar
visit (n.)	visita

English	*Portuguese*
vouch for	fiar (2)
waistline	cintura
wait for	esperar
waken	despertar
walk (v.)	andar
wall	parede
want (v.)	querer
warlike	bélico
warm	morno
warmth	calor
water	água
wave (n.)	onda
way	jeito
weapon	arma
wear	usar
weather	tempo (2)
week	semana
weeping (n.)	choro
weigh	pesar
well (adv.)	bem
well (interj.)	ora
wheel (n.)	roda
when	quando
which	qual
who	quem
why?	por quê
wind (n.)	vento
window	janela
wing (of a bird)	asa
wing (of a building)	ala
wink (v.)	piscar
wish (v.)	querer
with	com
without	sem
wood	mata

English	Portuguese
English	*Portuguese*
wool	lã
work of art	obra
world	mundo
worm (any unspecified)	bicho
worse	pior
wound (v.)	ferir
wounded	ferido
wrath	ira
year	ano
yes	sim
yesterday	ontem
yet	ainda
yokel	caipira
young man	rapaz
younger	menor

Printed and bound by CPI Group (UK) Ltd, Croydon, CR0 4YY

09/06/2025

14685839-0005